In Training for Reigning

A Testimony to God's faithfulness and provision

REG GARDNER

As told to Wendy Everingham

Some Scripture taken from the New King James Version®. Copyright © 1982 by Thomas Nelson. Used by permission. All rights reserved.

Some Scriptures are from the Holy Bible, New International Version® Anglicized, NIV® Copyright © 1979, 1984, 2011 by Biblica, Inc.® Used by permission. All rights reserved worldwide.

Some Scriptures and additional materials quoted are from the Good News Bible © 1994 published by the Bible Societies/HarperCollins Publishers Ltd UK, Good News Bible© American Bible Society 1966, 1971, 1976, 1992. Used with permission

Copyright © 2021 Reg Gardner & Wendy Everingham.

All rights reserved.

Cover design by Frances Everingham

Book design by Wendy Everingham

Contact us by email InTrainingForReigning@gmail.com

No part of this book can be reproduced in any form or by written, electronic or mechanical, including photocopying, recording, or by any information retrieval system without written permission in writing by the author.

Published by EverWendles

Printed by Book Printing UK www.bookprintinguk.com
Remus House, Coltsfoot Drive, Peterborough, PE2 9BF

Printed in Great Britain

Although every precaution has been taken in the preparation of this book, the publisher and author assume no responsibility for errors or omissions. Neither is any liability assumed for damages resulting from the use of information contained herein.

ISBN 978-1-5272-9788-3

A foreword plus three

Wendy Everingham
February 2021

I first met Reg in May 2019. My husband Sparra and I were on a trip to Israel with my church, Kingdom Faith London. My husband does not share my faith yet and I was a bit worried beforehand whether he would enjoy the trip with all my church friends. There were other people in the group that were not from my church and Reg was one of them. I firmly believe that Reg was sent by divine appointment to be on that trip. He hit it off with Sparra and they spent a lot of time together.

Reg reminds me of Del Boy from Only Fools and Horses for those of you that remember that series from the BBC. He is cheeky but full of the love of the Lord. Uncompromising in his faith, full of stories and anecdotes, many of which are in this book.

Another reason for my belief that Reg was a divine appointment was how I have come to write this book with him. At the time of writing, we are in our third lockdown due to the Covid-19 pandemic. I have always had an idea in the back of my mind that I would like to write a book but never knew where to start. Reg put a message on

Facebook to see if anyone could help him and I offered my services. Well, my first message was could we talk about it, but the first time I met him, Reg being Reg said have you got a computer? I had taken my laptop with me and he said ok shall we start then!! He didn't ask what my experience was or anything! We have both trusted God in this and hope that you enjoy the result, and it gives you some food for thought. It has helped us both through this period of lockdown!

  We serve an awesome God, and His ways are not our ways, but He does indeed have a plan and purpose for us if we would but trust Him.

Reg & Sparra, Israel 2019

Rev. Dave Gill
Senior Pastor

River Church
Canning Town

I have had the pleasure and joy of working with Reg for the best part of 25 years now. The first time I met him was when I arrived at our current church to be the new minister, his first question to this young pastor was "are you born again?". This question has always been Reg's passion and priority as it flows from his desire to see people saved and set free. From Reg's first encounter with the risen Jesus he has sought to draw people to the Lord who saved him and transformed his life. From the streets of Canning Town to the far reaches of West Africa and South America he has carried the same passion and hunger - to seek and save the lost and bring transformation into their lives. Reg has become more than a street preacher, though he still carries this anointing. He has become an agent of change in people's lives, bringing more than just a message of salvation. Reg has been used by Jesus to liberate people trapped in situations of poverty and desperation through his generosity of spirit and action working together.

Working with Reg has at times been a rollercoaster ride in which highs and lows, success and failures all play their part. The challenges he has faced, occasionally of his own creation, should not be discounted. For in Reg, like the Apostle Paul before him we conclude that "God has put his treasure in a jar of clay", that the glory and power of Jesus should be clearly demonstrated. I love Reg dearly and thank God that he has been part of my church for all these years as he has been one who will not sit back and be idle but recognises that the days are short so we must be about the work of the Lord.

As I reflect on the years past I come to the conclusion that every church should have a 'Reg'. In truth not every church would want one, or if they did would probably try to remove his rough edges and dampen his fire, but that would be a mistake. As you read his message, the story of his life, Reg's His-story, you will begin to see the hand of God at work. The passion for Jesus, the way that God redeems every situation and directs his path abundantly demonstrates not only the love Reg has for the Lord but the love the Lord has for him. I pray as you read this book you may catch something of the same Love, the same passion, the same desire for Jesus that Reg has and come to understand what it means to be "born again". To begin that new life in relationship with Jesus and join him in fulfilling the commission to go and make disciples of all nations.

Alan Craig,
Director of the Mayflower Family Centre in Canning Town, 1996 to 2003

There is only one Reg Gardner. Street trader to street preacher, his life story is fascinating.

I first met Reg when he arrived in Canning Town in London's docklands and then the most deprived neighbourhood in the country. Bold, restless, down to earth and sold out for God, I saw straight away that Reg had something different to offer the working-class locals – different, that is, from the usual middle-class Christian interlopers like me.

This was confirmed one Friday evening when we were sitting in the White House pub on Rathbone Street. Mid-evening, the band had a break from providing the usual entertainment. Reg leapt up, grabbed the mic and started to preach the Gospel to the surprised pub patrons. I don't think anyone was converted, but at least, as Reg might say, the word of salvation went forth and they heard the truth there is in Christ Jesus. When they come face-to-face with their Maker, the drinkers at the pub that night can't complain that no-one told ever them the way to heaven or how to avoid hell.

This book is Reg's story. Like I said, it is fascinating. I warmly commend it and him.

Peter Churchill –
Church without Walls

I have known Reggie for over 15 years. He is a one off, one of God's special characters, an evangelist and a man who tells it like it is. We came across a tract with two characters in it which we identified with in an uncanny way. This was confirmation to us that we should be working together on the street. Reggie is a man who always went for it and there are plenty of examples in this book. When you are prepared to step out and obey God the adventure is exhilarating and sometimes a bit scary. This is what this book is all about.

CONTENTS

Page

INTRODUCTION　　　　　　　　　　　　　　1

Chapter 1
HOW IT ALL BEGAN　　　　　　　　　　　3

Chapter 2
TIME IN KENT　　　　　　　　　　　　　　10

Chapter 3
GROWING UP　　　　　　　　　　　　　　13

Chapter 4
CANNING TOWN　　　　　　　　　　　　17

Chapter 5
MISSION TO WEST INDIES　　　　　　　29

Chapter 6
MISSION TO GUYANA　　　　　　　　　　43

Chapter 7
BREAD OF LIFE – CHURCH WITHOUT WALLS　　56

Contents (Continued)

Chapter 8
MISSION TO AFRICA   60

Chapter 9
MISSION TO ISRAEL   70

Chapter 10
MISSION TO NORTHERN IRELAND   86

Chapter 11
MISSION TO LITHUANIA   89

Chapter 12
RECENT ADVENTURES   92

Chapter 13
REFLECTIONS ON 30 YEARS OF SERVICE   95

INTRODUCTION

The ministry is like that of John the Baptist, based on Matthew 3 vs 3 and Isaiah 40 vs 3. *'A voice of one crying in the wilderness, prepare the way of the Lord'.* It is wonderful how the Lord allows us to walk through the scriptures on His highway of holiness. ***A highway shall be there, and a road, and it shall be called the Highway of Holiness. (Isaiah 35:8 NKJV).*** As I look back over my life I can see how the Lord leads us! My name is Reggie, of London, a sent one. Sent to the poor, the needy, the homeless and the rejects of society. But also, as the Bread of Life Church without Walls called to pull down the partitions between the denominations. We are called to look after the brethren who are on the mission field *'The harvest is plentiful, but the workers are few.' (Matthew 9:37 NIV).* Jesus said ***Truly I tell you, whatever you did for one of the least of these brothers and sisters of mine, you did for me.' (Matthew 25:40 NIV).*** I have never seen the righteous forsaken or their children begging for bread.

We don't give hands out we give hands up. Give them a fish and they eat the fish, give them a fishing rod - they learn to fish for themselves. People don't care how much we know until they know how much we care. *Let your light shine before men, that they may see your good works, and glorify your Father in Heaven. (Matthew 5:16 NIV).*

The Lord has called me to share in modern day parables, simple stories used to give a spiritual message. *So was fulfilled what was spoken through the prophet: "I will open my mouth in parables, I will utter things hidden since the creation of the world." (Matthew 13:35 NIV)* To reveal a hidden meaning as in Pilgrim's Progress of a spiritual journey with a promise of salvation as we all need a Saviour. Like Pilgrim in John Bunyan's Pilgrim's Progress, our steps are ordered by the Lord. *(Psalm 37:23 NKJV).*

Chapter 1

HOW IT ALL BEGAN

It all began in October 1990 with a phone call from my daughter Deborah. "Dad, I have met with Jesus". Part of me was happy but another part of me was wary. I was suspicious of what she was getting involved in! There are a lot of crackpots in the world, and I didn't realise I was one of them.

Go down to the potter's house, and there I will give you my message.' So I went down to the potter's house, and I saw him working at the wheel. But the pot he was shaping from the clay was marred in his hands; so the potter formed it into another pot, shaping it as seemed best to him. (Jeremiah 18:2-4 NIVUK)

On the following Sunday I travelled down to Snodland in Kent where I knew my daughter would be attending a Sunday service. There was a guy from America called Apostle Axel with the Pastor Andrew Perry, they led the meeting. I heard the words "Would anyone here like to give their lives to Jesus?" I was the only one there that wasn't a Christian. I just knew that if any man ever lived to show other men how to live that was Jesus, he was the Man! '

A few weeks before the phone call from my daughter, I had been driving down to Brighton to buy some jeans as stock for my market stall. A coach passed me and all the girls on board waved as they knew me because they worked in my second wife's factory on Canvey Island making skirts for British Home Stores. The thought went through my mind, that there must be more to life than this. The world tells you when you get this you will be happy, when you get that you will be happy. Here was I driving my Rolls Royce feeling as empty as hell. With all that I had, really, I had nothing, but I knew that there had to be something more to life than this. I had always believed in Jesus as a young boy, the problem was I used to say, "How come people are suffering, children are starving, and you are telling me that there is a Father in heaven that loves us!". I couldn't make it out – but I had never read the Bible!

My first wife was a very clever woman, and it was through her that I was set up in business as a market trader. Not only that she was the one that found a house in Swanley Village that had belonged to Captain Bligh of Mutiny on the Bounty fame. It had wine cellars underneath the house that I used to keep the stock in.

4

Captain Bligh was a famous Captain who had been put into a rowing boat by his crew and made to row back to England. All the crew became Christians I believe under a man called Mr Christian (strangely enough).

I had spent years on the so called high life but not knowing that I was lost and if I kept on going the way that I was going with thieving, being dishonest, not caring where the goods came from as long as the price was right. I could have gone to Hell. Thank the Lord He sees the heart!

At my daughter's church meeting, I heard one of the speakers say there were three people here that need to receive the gift of the Holy Spirit. Me, being me, thought, if there are any gifts on offer, I will have some. I quickly walked down the front to receive the gift. Now here I stood in front of these two Christians, Apostle Axel and Pastor Andrew Perry. I was the only one standing there and I got more than I expected!!! **The Spirit of the Sovereign LORD is on me, because the LORD has anointed me to proclaim good news to the poor. He has sent me to bind up the broken hearted, to proclaim freedom for the captives and release from darkness for the prisoners Isaiah 61 vs 1 (NIV)**

I started to speak in a language that I did not understand. I cried my eyes out as all the past hurts came to the surface. It was all part of the Lord's healing. As soon as they had finished praying for me, I couldn't wait to leave. It all seemed too spiritual for me. One man simply asked me my name! I said, "Forget it mate, I have only come down to see my daughter". I just got into my car and went home. I did not realise that I had been called of the Lord. *(You did not choose me, but I chose you John 15:16 NIV)*

When I arrived home, I didn't say anything to the wife. That night at 2 am I heard a voice say: "Get up, go downstairs and sit in your lounge". Three times it spoke to me ... because who wants to get up at 2 am! It was not an audible voice, but I knew that I had heard something deep within me. I had to respond! I got up went downstairs and sat in the lounge. This is what I heard:

"You are not of this world *(They are not of the world, just as I am not of the world John 17:16 NKJV)*. and this world is not of you …. Your body is a temple of the holy spirit *(Do you not know that your bodies are temples of the Holy Spirit, who is in you, whom you have received from God? You are not your own; 1 Corinthians 6:19 NIVUK)* and I want you to throw that rubbish in the bin."

At this time, I had an addiction that I had tried to give up many times. After hearing this command, I literally just threw it in the bin. I got up the next day and it wasn't until I went to bed in the evening, I realised I hadn't smoked anything. (I didn't even know I had been delivered from the addiction).

That night, again, at 2 am I heard the voice say: "get up, go downstairs and open the front door". Now that sounds whacky! But for some unknown reason it felt the right thing to do. I still didn't want to get up, but I did! I went down and opened the front door and two men walked in. I can't tell you what happened from there, the only thing I remember is that the next day I was out running, doing the morning exercise with the dog and I said to Jesus "I know that You came but who was the person with You?". He said, "it was the Father and I; we have come to make our home with you".

'Jesus replied, 'Anyone who loves me will obey my teaching. My Father will love them, and we will come to them and make our home with them.' John 14 vs 23. (NIV)

A few days after this I sat in my little office and I remember looking at a crucifix I had that had a little image on it of Jesus. I didn't feel very comfortable, I just felt that I should get rid of it. As I went to throw it in the bin, I felt in my spirit to take it back to the church. When I arrived at the church it was closed. I thought 'I know there is another church a ten-minute drive away I will go there'. Again, I found that was closed as well. I sat in the car feeling like I was going off my rocker, head in my hands!

I then felt the Lord say to me 'Reggie you can go home now'. I thought to myself 'What'? The Lord had set me free from a religious spirit because I had treated the crucifix as a holy relic, an idol. *You shall not make for yourself an image in the form of anything in heaven above or on the earth beneath or in the waters below. You shall not bow down to them or worship them; for I, the Lord your God, am a jealous God (Exodus 20 4-5a NIV).*

As I looked up … just across the road was a Christian bookshop! I decided to go in and buy a Bible. I asked the woman behind the counter if I could have a Bible, she said what kind of Bible would you like? I had no idea, so I went to the back of the shop and asked Jesus what one I should get. I felt in my spirit the Lord tell me to get a Good News Bible because it was in a language that I could understand. I have now graduated to the New King James Bible!

When I read in the Gospel of John chapter 14 vs 23, I was overwhelmed. Because there it was '*If you love me, you will keep my commandments and I and the*

Father will come to you and make our home with you'. (WOW!), I was so overwhelmed to think that God the Father of all creation along with Jesus had come to visit me!! Life would never be the same again.

Chapter 2

TIME IN KENT

I gave up my wheeling and dealing. I decided I was going to serve the Lord! With £250 in my pocket, I left everything behind like Pilgrim, in Pilgrim's Progress. The Lord took me into the wilderness to teach me His ways. He gave me a mobile home down at Wateringbury near Paddock Wood in Kent.

The Bible says if you don't work you don't eat. I had decided to fit smoke alarms to get into people's homes just to share the good news of the gospel. One particular week I hadn't earned any money. It got to Friday morning and the rent was due the following day. I was anxious! But the Bible says **'Be anxious for nothing, but in everything by prayer and supplication, with thanksgiving, let your requests be made known to God' (Philippians 4:6 NIV)** In one ear I heard 'if you don't work you don't eat' and in the other ear I heard 'stay in and read your Bible'. What do you do, as the devil can quote you scripture! Thank God for the Holy Spirit because I felt, in my spirit, that I should stay in and read my Bible. The enemy will never tell you to read your Bible I was being driven when I heard 'if you don't work you don't eat' ... I was being condemned. The Lord will never drive you He will lead you. Thank God for the Holy Spirit who will never condemn you but will convict you *(Therefore, there is now no condemnation for those who are in Christ Jesus, Romans 8:1 NIVUK)* ... there is a difference. As I read my Bible, the phone rang and it was the director of Brett's Bananas, Graham Lucas, in Kent. He said, "Reg I know you used to drive a big car and I have lost my license so can you drive me to London in my Lexus for a meeting?" I knew, with him being a millionaire, I was going to be ok for my rent money!

As I put the phone down, I started to cry. I said, "Lord I can't live like this". It was too much tension! I felt the Lord say in my Spirit 'Reg you didn't have faith, you were hoping I would supply your needs, but you didn't have the faith to know that I would.' For faith is things hoped for that you cannot see, if you could see you wouldn't need faith. *'To have faith is to be sure of the things we hope for, to be certain of the things we cannot see.' (Hebrews 11 vs 1)* God's work, done God's way, gets God's supply.

The battle was on, but the battle belongs to the Lord. '.. *for the battle is not yours, but God's (2*

Chronicles 20:15 NIV)). Unless the Lord builds a house the builders labour in vain. (Psalm 127 vs 1 NIV). You must be born again to have a new life and a new spirit. ***Jesus replied, "I tell you the truth, unless you are born again, you cannot see the Kingdom of God." (John 3 vs 3 NLT)*** You MUST be born again. I had been born again.

While I lived in the caravan, I went to the Sheepfold church in Maidstone. This church specialised in healing and deliverance. They had a wonderful teaching ministry. Authority is greater than power, for example a 5ft 7 policeman, a 20 ton truck coming down the road it could flatten him. But he has the authority of the Queen of England. If he stands in the road and puts his hand up, he has the authority to stop that truck! How much more when we say stop! We have the authority of the Lord of Lords and the King of Kings and all the Heavenly hosts.

Chapter 3

GROWING UP

I was born in London of Irish parents at the end of the 1930's. I grew up very much on my own. Never had much of a home life as I was left on the street like most kids playing on the bomb sites in those days. I went to school in the clothes I slept in. I am not saying we were poor but even the mice gave the cheese back. I went to a church school and that is where I first heard the gospel, I didn't realise then that a seed had been sown. I remember two things *'What profits a man if he gains the whole world but suffers the loss of his soul' (Mark 8:36 NIV)* **and** *'Jesus said: I am the Way, the Truth and the Life'. (John 14:6 NIV)*

My parents were always fighting and smashing things up, shouting at each other. I remember my father being drunk and crying for his wife, my mother, because she had left us. I was only young. I felt so sorry for my father. They never hit me but there are other kinds of cruelty that children can go through in a dysfunctional family. It is a curse because I ended up doing the same things to my first wife. I was under a curse, but I never knew it. I used to shout and rave at her, and it affected my children. Hurt people hurt people. This is what is known as a generational curse that comes through the family line. Curses such as this must be broken through prayer and forgiveness. Forgive those who have hurt you and let them go because it is not a feeling it is an act of your will. You must choose to forgive. If you go on your feelings, you will never forgive.

The modern day parable of the naughty monkey illustrates this. A missionary in Africa goes into a village and all the people are upset because there is a naughty monkey that comes in and steals all their food. 'What shall we do?' said the people, so the missionary told them to get a jar and put some nuts at the bottom. Then put it into the ground so that it could not be pulled out, then watch what would happen when the naughty monkey came along. So, all the people hid out of sight and as the monkey came down the street, he spots the jar with the nuts. So, what does he do? He puts his hand in the jar and grabs a handful of nuts. But he can't get his hand out because he won't let go of the nuts! Sometimes we are like that naughty monkey, we don't want to let go and forgive those that have hurt us. We all need prayer because who hasn't been hurt! We have all been hurt.

But the Lord's Prayer says that you must forgive. **'Forgive us the wrongs we have done, as we forgive the wrongs that others have done to us' (Matt 6 vs 12' GNB).**

In the 1950's my National Service came up when we had to enlist in either the Army, Navy or the RAF. I chose the RAF because I thought it would be a cushy number!! I'd had no education as such, but I was streetwise like the Artful Dodger, from Oliver Twist, so they put me in the Stores. We kitted out the recruits with everything they needed to start their stint in National Service. I had worked in the men's clothing business before I started my National Service, so I had previous experience! After I left school, I had chosen that line of work because I wanted to wear nice shirts and suits because of my scruffy background. Going into the RAF for National Service gave me a glimpse of a better way of life.

I met my first wife in the RAF at the Camp dance. A beautiful girl and a wonderful mother just as the Bible states in Proverbs 31 vs 10 – 31. *A wife of noble character who can find. She is worth far more than rubies (Proverbs 31 vs 10 NIV).* I wish I knew then what I know now. I would have treated her a lot better. The good news is she also became a Christian.

God choses your family, you chose your friends. I once asked the Lord why I was left filthy, dirty and stinking as a young lad, with bed sheets that hadn't been washed for years. We didn't even have electricity, only an oil lamp. He spoke to me and said 'Reg I have called you to the homeless, the needy and the rejects to reach out with a heart of compassion because you can share from the heart and not from the head as you know exactly how they feel'.

If you want to be like Jesus believe me, you will share in His suffering. Mary and Joseph had travelled to Bethlehem. Joseph must have had family in Bethlehem but for some reason there was no room for them to stay at the inn! They were homeless. Jesus was born in a stable. It would not have been a very nice place! All this shows how He identifies with people who are homeless and needy. *For I was hungry and you gave me something to eat, I was thirsty and you gave me something to drink, I was a stranger and you invited me in (Matthew 25 vs 35 NIV)*

Chapter 4

CANNING TOWN

Two years later I found myself in Canning Town serving the Seer, Pastor Johnny Barr, who was from a gypsy family. I first heard him speak at Brooksby Christian Camp and that is when I decided to join his church. Johnny had been teaching on demonic influences and territorial spirits. He had an itinerant ministry working with David Pawson and Derek Prince. He also had his own deliverance ministry every month at his own church. The first words Johnny ever spoke to me were 'Welcome brother we have been expecting you'. I think he was expecting more than what he got! Helen Shapiro, who is a Messianic Jew, used to come on a regular basis and she had a hit song in the 1950's called 'Walking back to happiness'. A few years later she came to know the Lord and that song was really a prophetic one! She became a Christian about the same time as Sir Cliff Richard who went on to give a testimony at a Billy Graham Crusade in the 1960's. Billy Graham was one of the greatest evangelists of the 20th Century. He has now gone to be with the Lord!

I was baptised at Brooksby in 1991. That was the first time that I gave my testimony of deliverance from addiction before I went down into the water. As I came up out of the water, I felt I had been washed clean! This is just what Cliff Richard also said when he was baptised by David Pawson.

So here I was in Canning Town. Johnny was the Pastor of an Elim church. I liked Canning Town as it had a good market in those days. I could identify with the traders being a market man myself. I used to hand out gospel tracts.

Near the Elim Church was a place called the Mayflower Centre. The Mayflower Centre has a wonderful history that stretches back 125 years. 125 years of reaching the poor and needy. The director of the Mayflower Centre, Alan Craig, came to me and asked if I would do some evangelising for them. I said "Yes' if my Pastor Johnny Barr agrees". Johnny called me into the office and said "Reg, I want you to go and be a bridge from our church to the Mayflower Centre". So, I went. A couple of years later the Lord took Johnny home to be with Him and the rest of the congregation followed me to the Mayflower. They renamed the Mayflower Centre the River Christian Church. It was first established at the site it is still on as the Malvern Mission in 1894. Canning

Town was known as one of the most deprived areas of the East End of London from 1895 - 2005. In 1923 it became known as the Dockland Settlements No 1. There was another name change in 1958 to the Mayflower Centre. David Sheppard, who was a famous cricketer was the Pastor at the time. These are our roots as we have continued to preach the good news to the poor in the marketplace and underneath the flyover opposite Canning Town station serving hot drinks and sandwiches from our market stall. A logo on the front reads 'The Bread of Life, come and taste and see that the Lord is good'. ***Oh, taste and see that the LORD is good; Blessed is the man who trusts in Him! (Psalm 34:8 NKJV)*** Today Canning Town is now one of the most expensive places to live in London with London City Airport and the Excel Centre close by. This is all history, but in fact it is 'His' story!! Jesus has always had a heart for the poor in the East End of London.

When I arrived at the Mayflower, I met a friend of Johnny's by the name of Bryan Church. A wonderful man who gave out Gideon Bibles to schools and hospitals. He is still a good friend of mine today, as he keeps me on the straight and narrow!

The River Church Christian Centre follows the principles of Matthew 25. ***The King will reply, 'I tell you,*** *whenever you did this for one of the least important of these followers of mine, you did it for me! (Matt 25 vs 40 GNT)'* I wasn't surprised when the Lord sent me here as I was one of those kids that used to play on the bombsites and get filthy dirty. But we were never sick as we grew up with strong immune systems, not like today where there is a spray for everything. My Mum used to say that it was clean dirt. Work that one out!

In Canning Town market from the 1990's every Good Friday Alan Craig, the director of the Mayflower Centre (as it was called in those days) used to hire an open back truck so that we could preach the good news of the gospel of Jesus. On Good Friday it was always packed with lots of people, buying fruit, veg and fresh fish. You could even buy fresh rabbits in those days! One Good Friday we went into the market, but we were asked to leave because of political correctness. Yet the laws and justice of this country are based on Christian principles! The good news is the Newham Recorder (the local newspaper) printed a letter I wrote to them with the headline 'No market for Gospel' (see article). What the enemy planned for bad the Lord turned to good as it must have been seen by thousands more people than would have been there on market day!

No market for Gospel

I'M an ex-market trader who came to Canning Town in 1993. Since then I have been sharing the good news of the Gospel.

When I came to know the Lord Jesus I was set free from drug addiction which changed my life. What He's done for me He'll do for others.

Last Good Friday, for the first time ever, me and my friends were told not to sing and to remove a cross as it was 'an offence' to other people. Yet for over 100 years traders and locals have been given free stalls as we celebrate Easter! Jesus Himself was always in the market place, according to the Bible.

The laws of this land are based on Christian principles and I was very surprised and disappointed to experience discrimination. Where has our freedom gone? – **REG GARDNER, Vincent Street, Canning Town.**

Alan Craig, Benny Stafford and myself stood in the local elections for the People's Christian Alliance and Alan got elected as a local Councillor on Newham Council.

There were changes in the pipeline at River Church. It was part of God's plan for Roger Grassham to become the senior pastor. His knowledge as a civil engineer and his knowledge of how Newham Council works has been instrumental in the successful signing of an agreement to have the site of the River Church Centre redeveloped. When it is completed there will be affordable housing and a conference centre amongst other things. It has taken 12 years to be finally agreed. The church stays because it has a preservation order on it as does my place which is next door. It used to be Pastor David's flat. The church will have everything it needs for the future.

Pastor David Gill's vision is to send missionaries around world. *For I know the plans I have for you,' declares the Lord, 'plans to prosper you and not to harm you, plans to give you hope and a future. Then you will call on me and come and pray to me, and I will listen to you. You will seek me and find me when you seek me with all your heart. (Jeremiah 29:11- 13 NIV).* Pastor David Gill actually stepped aside to let Roger be Senior Pastor as he realised that was God's plan at the time. He is the only man that I have ever met in 30 years who laid aside his ministry as a senior pastor to allow the Macedonian call '*And a vision appeared to Paul in the night. A man of Macedonia stood and pleaded with him, saying, "Come over to Macedonia and help us." (Acts 16:9 NKJV)*'. He had to step aside to allow someone else be senior pastor for a time to build God's Work. As he said to me when I questioned why he was standing down 'but this is God's Church and not my church!' This is the sign of a true man of God! Can you live with no recognition, no reputation, and no position! If you can't then it's not God's ministry. But David did get the church back later, bigger and better than it had been in the first place. *The Lord restored the fortunes of Job when he prayed for his friends, and the Lord gave Job twice as much as he had before. (Job 42:10 AMP).*

Canning Town has been my home now for over 25 years and the place I come back to when I have been away on mission. I have also had the chance to serve here as well. On one occasion Benny Hinn came to London to lead healing meetings at the Excel Exhibition Centre. It gave me the chance to look and reflect on how the Lord works out His healing in people's lives. I noticed that it was through the worship that people were being healed and the Holy Spirit confirmed with signs and wonders following. This all had to do with the prayer that had been invested into the meeting.

It has not always been easy being part of the church here and I believe the Lord wants me to talk about the difficulties that I have experienced over the years that has made me disappointed and discouraged. *"I have told you these things, so that in me you may have peace. In this world you will have trouble. But take heart! I have overcome the world." (John 16 vs 33 NIVUK).'*. I cannot speak for all of us, but I feel the Lord has put me in the church to die to self. *'He himself bore our sins' in his body on the cross, so that we might die to sins and live for righteousness; 'by his wounds you have been healed.'(1 Peter 2 vs 24 NIVUK).* As a Market Trader I was very well placed to be an evangelist with the 'gift of the gab'. Speaking on the street comes easily to me.

24

My first invitation to join the ministry was as an evangelist to the local church. I found myself in a situation that was difficult as the office was running the church instead of the church running the office. The crunch came when we opened the sports centre for the homeless with two other churches coming in to help. The office didn't like me, and the manager tried to stop me as he was in charge of the site. He accused me of upsetting the homeless, you won't believe that, as I was talking about Jesus! The place was full of smoke and they were watching television. It was a dreadful situation. I was gutted and disappointed that even the other churches that came into help didn't say anything! I got so wounded in my spirit that it made me feel physically sick. The world says that 'sticks and stones may break your bones, but names will never hurt you' but that is a lie from the pit! Have you ever had someone say something to you that hit you and made you upset? I decided to write five letters to the directors of the organisation as it was supposed to be a Christian outreach and I had been asked to come in as an evangelist to share the good news of the Bible to those in need. I remember lying on the floor crying out to the Lord as I was so disappointed and felt that I had failed and maybe wasn't called to be an evangelist. As I lay on the floor, I felt the Lord say to me 'would you offer me something that has cost you nothing?' These words got me up off the floor as I decided there and then that I was going to carry on. I gave the letters to Pastor David to give to the leaders and directors of the Christian Centre. I waited two or three weeks and as I had not had a response, I asked Pastor David what had happened. He told me 'Reg, I didn't give them the letters because you were so upset it would have just put more wood on the fire which needed to go out'. Not long after the Lord then took me away on mission to the Caribbean which was a great experience. On my return to the UK, I found that all the people that were against me the Lord had removed! They were no longer there. Sometimes the Lord has to take us out of the situation as we cannot accomplish anything in the flesh of the old carnal nature. **'Not by might not by power but my spirit says the Lord'. (Zechariah 4 vs 6 NIV).** For the Lord defends us and gives us victory **(1 John 5 vs 4).** It is all about forgiveness. What good is it if you only love those that love you **(Luke 6 vs 32 – 36).** Even though I had been wounded by so many in the body of Christ we still carry on **(John 16 vs 33).** 'Persevere do not give up'. At that time, I did not want to go on Mission as I was feeling 'Woe is me' sorry for myself. I was feeling my age! I wasn't feeling good enough until the Lord spoke to me and said, 'Reg you are undermining the Cross' As I was coming under condemnation. **Therefore, there is now no** *condemnation for those who are in Christ Jesus, (Romans 8 vs 1)*. So off I went again as the Lord's Ambassador as part of His Special Forces one of the Lord's paratroopers. Just like the SAS or the SWAT teams in the U.S. The weapons of our warfare are not carnal but mighty for the pulling down of strongholds! *Zechariah 4 vs 6. 'Not by might not by power but by my spirit says the Lord'* it is so important to be covered by a group of believers that will keep you under a covering of prayer. As in the book of Acts they met together on a regular basis. How can you be in fellowship if you have no relationship? Without prayer cover, we would be in serious trouble. (We do get hurt so it is important to get prayer for healing and have people around you that you can trust to pray for you for protection) In Israel the officers go before the men to lead them into battle this is why as leaders they get hurt as they lead by example. They never leave their wounded behind and will keep the whole group together in unity so that they all get home safe. The wounded need prayer for healing as there is an enemy out there that wants to steal, kill and destroy. Have a read of John 10 vs 10 – 29. There are no Lone Rangers in the body of Christ, as even the Lone Ranger had Tonto and we need one another. For it is not about our ministry and looking after ourselves as the gospel is not for peddling, freely we receive, freely give. *As you go, proclaim this message: 'The kingdom of heaven has come near.' 'Heal the sick, raise the dead, cleanse those who have leprosy, drive out demons. Freely you have received; freely give.' (Matthew 10 vs 5 – 8)*

Raising the dead is not always physical. As it has more of a spiritual connotation. Luke 9 vs 60 says ***'Let the dead bury their own dead'(NIVUK).*** That is why salvation is so important to bring others from death to life. ***Matthew 28 vs 18 – 20. Then Jesus came to them and said, 'All authority in heaven and on earth has been given to me. Therefore go and make disciples of all nations, baptising them in the name of the Father and of the Son and of the Holy Spirit, and teaching them to obey everything I have commanded you. And surely I am with you always, to the very end of the age'. (NIVUK)***

Chapter 5

MISSION TO WEST INDIES

In 2003 the Lord took me to the West Indies. I met a pastor at a prayer meeting lead by Georgie Strange (who got born again in prison). This chap invited me to go to the West Indies, but I told him I had no desire to go back to that old life as I had been to the Caribbean many times before I knew Jesus. He said there was plenty of work there for the Gospel. I didn't realise the only reason he wanted me to go with him was to share the expenses! But what the enemy meant for bad the Lord turned for good. Thank God for Georgie Strange! As he said to me, 'Reg you have already been called to go into the prisons with me and Es Kaitell, so this trip is just an extension of that'. Es has a wonderful testimony. He had a background in security work and worked as a bodyguard. He used to be involved with specialist protection and has written a book called 'Let me ask you nicely', which I highly recommend. It tells the story of how the Lord replaced the steel in his head after he had been beaten up by a gang with baseball bats! He was determined to kill the guys who had attacked him. However, on his way to get revenge he met two Christians who took him to a meeting at Kensington Temple with his wife where he got saved as the Lord healed him. The two Christians he went to the meeting with told him that he had to forgive those that had hurt him, but that is not exactly what he had in mind. But thank the Lord that He sees the heart!

As I said, we had already been working in prisons in the UK, regularly visiting HMP Blundeston. So, Georgie Strange got in touch with Prison Fellowship International. Thank the Lord he did because the Pastor who invited me didn't know anybody and didn't have any connections in the ministry!! Prison Fellowship International was founded by Chuck Colson of Watergate fame (he was one of President Nixon's aides). As he served his prison sentence for corruption, he realised that the prisoners and their families were in dire need. So, he introduced the Angel Tree at Christmas for prisoners' children. This way children would get a present each Christmas from their parent who was serving time. The tree is placed in places such as supermarkets and shopping centres where people can leave a gift wrapped present and write on the gift tag shaped like an angel whether the gift is for a girl or boy.

I was soon on my way to Barbados. Thomas Watts, the director of Prison Fellowship International there, met us at the airport. He said, 'Reg you are coming with me to the prisons around the Caribbean'. What a wonderful first assignment, I thought I was in paradise! Barbados, St Lucia, St Kitts, Nevis, and St Vincent. The only problem was I had no money! Pastor Watts just chuckled when I told him and said we are still going! I remember we went to this place called the Captain's Cabin and we booked in. I knew we didn't have any money! I said to him 'we can't stay here… I am going to have to go and tell the woman in charge'. Pastor Watts, again, just chuckled … 'Lady' I said, 'we have no money'. She said, 'As you are missionaries, you can stay here, and I will feed you every day'. She also took us to the local radio station where we were able to share the good news to the people on the island! God's work, done God's way gets God's supply. I still had to learn *(I will instruct you and teach you in the way you should go; I will guide you with My eye. Psalm 32 :8 NIV)*

When we travelled to St Vincent, the prison at that time was in the centre of the town. We went to meet the Prison governor, a man by the name of Rodriguez. As he sat in his office, he told us he was fed up with people coming in and 'upsetting his prisoners with religion'. As a guest and invited by two other ministers I asked for permission to speak. The Lord had given me a word straight from His Throne Room for Rodriguez, "Sir, The Lord has heard your prayer." Nobody knew that this man was in fact a Pastor as well as Governor. "Sir" I said, "I would like to see your prisoners". He called in his first officer, Brenan, and told him to show me around the prison.

The prisoners were all in cages. How would you feel as a black man if a white man came up to look at you in a cage! I said "Stop, I would like to see them all together in the yard!" They told me to come back at 7 am the next morning. I had no idea how I would get to the prison the next day, but as usual the Lord provided as one of the prison officers lived near where I was staying and gave me a lift! So, the next day I stood in the yard on some steps and shared with the inmates. Twenty-nine accepted the gospel on my first visit and thirty seven when I went back again. That makes 66 in total … the same number as there are books in the Bible. We have a picture of the men as a testimony to God's goodness. Normally nobody is allowed to take photos of the prisoners, but by God's grace it was allowed on this occasion. Now Rodriguez had 66 souls to look after as pastor and Governor! That is the God we serve!

Prisoners in St Vincent's Prison after I preached the gospel

It is amazing how the Lord works in our lives. When I had returned to Barbados, I still had no money of my own for food or anything else. I was staying in a converted garage with a bed, shower, and a kitchen; it was nicer than it sounds! Then afterwards I found out that I couldn't get any money out of the bank, so I had to tell them I was sorry, but I couldn't afford to pay the rent. This was the second time that this had happened! But they said to me 'It's ok, that's not a problem'. Another example of God's work, done God's way getting God's supply.

Pastor Watts had given me a frozen chicken to do with whatever I wanted. I had to travel from Bridgetown in Barbados back to Kirtons where I was staying. It was about a 45-minute bus journey. I had my bus fare and there I was sat on the bus with a frozen chicken. A woman came and sat next to me; her name was Jean. We started to chat, and it turned out that she was also travelling to Kirtons. I explained to her that I was a missionary and living in the same district. She responded that she also was a Christian. (In the West Indies most people claim to be Christians). I told her that I didn't know what to do with the frozen chicken. She told me to give it to her and she would make sure that I had something to eat every day. Again, God had it all under control! She invited me to go to the cathedral with her the next Sunday. When some-one says 'cathedral' you expect an enormous stone building, but this was just a large building with a tin roof! Not quite what I had in mind! After the meeting she wanted to introduce me to this man, called Samuel. When I met him, he asked me if I had a need in any area. As an Englishman I wasn't telling anyone! Pride!!! The things that God has to deal with in us! I wasn't telling him that I didn't have any money, I simply said to him 'Thank you very much I am fine'. I was defensive. As I walked away the Lord said to me 'I want you to go back to him because I need you to go back to St Vincent to the prisoners you have just visited'. This was when another 37 prisoners made a commitment to the Lord. It is a plane ride from Barbados to St Vincent and I had to tell Samuel that I did not have any money. So, I turned round and went back to Samuel. I said, 'Excuse me sir, but I have got to go back to St Vincent.' He said 'ok, where are you staying?' That evening he visited me and as I opened the door, Samuel said 'The Lord told me that you were coming'. I thought that was encouraging! Then he started to cry, He said, 'I knew there was something different about this place, because a girl who had lived in this house had been kidnapped, killed and thrown into a well.' So, Samuel gave me the money to go back to the prison on St Vincent with Owen Williams who I had met through Pastor Watts.

Owen Williams was the director of the Bible Society for the West Indies and had an office in Bridgetown, Barbados which he let me use. He supplied the books that we were able to give to the newly saved prisoners. Owen had a cousin that I later met on the replica slave ship The Zong that was berthed on the Thames at the Tower of London in 2007. Clifford and

Monica Hill had arranged for it to be brought up to the Thames to celebrate the 200th Anniversary of William Wilberforce's emancipation of the slave trade. The ship showed man's inhumanity to man! I was invited to speak to the visitors in the coffee shop before they left after they had spent time on the ship. Amazing Grace was the name of the film that came out at the same time as the slave ship was berthed at the Tower of London. The film told the story of William Wilberforce and his campaign to get slavery banned.

.I did a television interview while I was in St Vincent's and I spoke on their slave heroes like Cuffy and Bussa. They were slaves that had led slave revolts. On the television programme I said that I could see statues of Nelson etc around the islands but not statues of heroes like Cuffy and Bussa. Nelson had been against the emancipation of the slave trade. I informed them that because their blood had been shed on the land the Lord had honoured that spilled blood. I said that the Lord had given them these wonderful islands as an inheritance to own and govern. The Caribbean is one of the most beautiful places in the world.

Above   Owen Williams of Bible Society

Below: Reg with Thomas Watts from Prison Fellowship International

Through Samuel, I also got to visit a psychiatric hospital in Barbados. I came across a patient called Brenda who was telling the other inmates all about Jesus. Brenda had trained to be a teacher then had a mental break down. She was released after a while but then a few years later I heard she had been readmitted to the same hospital. I had to ask the Lord why he would allow one of his children back into a psychiatric hospital and I felt the Lord say, 'She is reaching more people being an inmate than being on the outside'. There are some things that I find difficult to understand. Like Brenda in the psychiatric hospital her experiences helped her to share the good news with the other patients. My experiences as a poor, scruffy child had prepared me for the work with the homeless later in my life. *For I know the plans I have for you to prosper you and not to harm you to give you a future and a hope. (Jeremiah 29 vs 11 – 13).*

It was amazing how we found favour with the authorities of the psychiatric hospital in Barbados. *Then you will win favour and a good name in the sight of God and man. (Proverbs 3:4 NIVUK).* The Lord got us into every part of the exceptionally large complex to share the good news of the gospel. Men and women in different stages of mental health, living in separate sections, depending on the severity of their illness. The amazing power of the Holy Spirit and the Word of Dr Jesus. We were able to show the love of Christ, with a touch. One of the songs we used to sing in the women's ward was 'Because of who you are we give you glory'. This brought tears to my eyes as the women gathered around. It was such a wonderful experience, feeling the presence of the Lord that I will never forget!

Again, as I look back and reflect, I realise that the apostolic ministry is not a title, but a calling. Altogether we spent five years reaching out in the Caribbean around the various Islands. To the prisoners with Angel Tree gifts for the children, to those in need in the town's local hospital by praying for the sick. The song always comes to mind with the words "Jesus makes a way, where there seems to be no way" *See, I am doing a new thing! Now it springs up; do you not perceive it? I am making a way in the wilderness and streams in the wasteland (Isaiah 43 vs 19 NIVUK).*

I had gone to the West Indies with the faith of Luke 9:3. '*And He said to them, "Take nothing for the journey, neither staffs nor bag nor bread nor money; and do not have two tunics apiece)" (NKJV).*' One time I visited Barbados the Lord sent Barbara an estate agent to supply a small villa for me to live in for no charge. The villa was near Sandy Lane Hotel where Tiger Woods the golfer got married. It is a large hotel complex for millionaires. They need saving as much as the poor. It is harder for them to come to Jesus. ***"And again, I say to you, it is easier for a camel to go through the eye of a needle than for a rich man to enter the kingdom of God." (Matthew 19 vs 24 NKJV).*** When we get born again it is like a romance, being in love with Jesus and it is beautiful like the Caribbean, which was the first assignment I had from the Lord!

On another occasion I had returned to Barbados after travelling around the islands of the Caribbean and Pastor Watts had found me somewhere to live with a Bishop. It was a small tin shack house with the Bishop, his wife and son. It was here that I was introduced to Pastor Melvin Smith and a guy called Earl. They invited me to go and meet the Rastafarians in Guyana. I agreed to go, as a Rasta to me is like a market trader – streetwise. I had already shared with the Rastafarians in the villages in Barbados. They are into drugs in a big way there. I would tell them this modern-day parable:

Every gang has a gang leader, with thieves wanting an easy, so called 'living'. Selling drugs and ill-gotten gains. If one member of one gang gets caught walking through another gang's territory, they 'mash him up', beat him up as a warning to not return. This happened to one guy as he walked through the wrong area and he suffered a serious beating. A friend came along and saw him lying on the floor. Thinking the gang had gone he went and picked him up. As he carried him away the gang returned and killed HIM! But he had saved his friend who he managed to rescue before he died! The boy that survived was a beautiful artist, he drew a picture of the lad who saved him. He took it to the father who lived on his own. When he knocked on the door the father opened the door and the boy asked him if he knew who he was. 'Yes', said the father, 'I know you; you are the boy that my son saved.' It was a beautiful picture and the father thanked him as he received it and the boy left. A few months later the father died. In his house there were valuable silver antiques, gold ornaments, and paintings all worth thousands. They had to have an auction; people came from everywhere. The first item up for sale was the picture of the man's son. 'We don't want that', they shouted, 'we have come for the gold and silver'. People weren't interested in it. The auctioneer said that he had been instructed to sell the picture of the man's son first. Right at the back of the crowd was the father's handyman who used to look after his garden and do repairs when they were needed. Up went his hand! He offered £10 or $15 in US money. No one else wanted the picture so it was sold to the handyman! Then the auctioneer declared that the auction was now over! The audience cried out 'What do you mean the auction is closed!' The auctioneer explained that the father loved the son so much that whoever bought the picture of his son had now inherited everything, the gold, silver, and antiques. Always at this point I would stop and ask those listening would you have liked to have been the handyman? The poor handyman is now a rich man. Again, I would pause and wait for a response. Now I had got their attention I would then go on to explain that the man who had been hurt and wounded was me. The man who came in and got me was Jesus. *The disciples came to him and asked, 'Why do you speak to the people in parables?' He replied, 'Because the knowledge of the secrets of the kingdom of heaven has been given to you, but not to them. (Matthew 13:10-11 NIVUK)* Because I love the son (Jesus) I have inherited the kingdom as the father owns all the gold and silver (Haggai 2 vs 8) so I am a rich man. I have never been short in 30 years. God's work, done God's way, gets God's supply. I have never seen the righteous forsaken or their children begging for bread.

Chapter 6

MISSION TO GUYANA

Off I went to Guyana expecting to go to the Rastas, but the Lord had other plans. Not for me to go to the Guyanan Rastafarians, but to meet a widow woman living in a swamp in Sophia with 8 orphan children. This was in an area called Kitty which had a statue of Cuffy the slave hero in the central square of the town. There were alligators crossing the road from one stream to the other which is an amazing sight to see!

I was soon up to my knees in the swamp. I killed one mosquito and a thousand came to the funeral! The widow's name was Amelia, and she is the mother of Melanie who had married our young Pastor David Gill. David received death threats when he had travelled to Guyana with his new wife to pay his respects to her family. Her brother Richard had been killed for $20, life is cheap in Guyana.

Pastor Melvin went with me because he wouldn't allow me to go into the swamp on my own. He knew the number of killings and murders that happen there. When

I met Amelia, I told her we needed to break bread and to build a wall of protection around her dwelling (one is spiritual protection, and one is natural protection). Harry Baldwin, one of the saints I worked with alongside Johnny Barr had told me before I left for Guyana to take the bread and wine. There was a lot of witchcraft around Amelia as Sophia is under a curse because a lot of slaves had been killed and their blood had been shed in the past.

After Richard had been killed everything had been stolen from Amelia. Whatever she had they would take. Richard had had a heart to feed the poor. Before we took the bread and wine, I had to ask Amelia to forgive those who had killed her children because another daughter had also died from a heart attack. Her words to me were 'I know their lives had a meaning' (that was why we were there). Pastor Melvin said 'I can see Richard standing with Jesus with some kind of tattoo on his arm' She told us that wasn't a tattoo but it was where they 'mashed' him up with a machete. Because his blood had been spilt the Lord had sent me to honour Amelia, because of his heart to feed the poor. In fact, we are still doing that today, and she feeds between 10 - 20 children two days a week.

The Lord had sent me to build a secure wall around the house and support the family. The wall took years to build because of the opposition of the enemy. Men fell sick, materials were stolen! I remember on leaving Guyana over 15 years ago I had given the money for the construction of the wall to Pastor Melvin Smith. For nearly a year I hadn't heard anything from Melanie's mother, Amelia, or Pastor Melvin. I was very concerned because it was a substantial amount of money! I decided to return and informed Pastor Melvin Smith I was coming! He met me at the airport with two other ministers I told them that I was not a happy bunny! As far as I knew no work had been carried out on the widow woman's home, so I had returned to find out what was going on! My first words were 'Where's the money?' and 'What has been happening?' This was the explanation that was given to me. Pastor Melvin said there was a builder in his congregation (a Christian) who he had asked to do the work. The builder went to the supplier and said to him if I give you the contract to supply the materials will you wipe out the money that I owe you? What was he doing? They were going to steal from the widow woman! The supplier would take the debt out of the building money. THEY BOTH DROPPED DEAD. These were not old men. The Bible tells us not to mistreat the widows and orphans it could cost you your life. *'Take care of orphans and widows in their suffering' (James 1:27 GNT)*, It was the Lord's money!!

As Christians these men never realised the consequences of their actions! Remember what happened to Ananias and Sapphira in Acts 5 vs 1 – 11. Have St Peter as your Pastor, lie about the offering and you soon get slain in the Spirit! It cost them their lives! Anyway, thank God for Pastor Melvin who undertook to finish the building of the wall for the widow woman. It took five years in the end to get Amelia safe and things sorted out.

My adventures in the West Indies and Guyana remind me of another parable that I like to tell which shows the importance of how we are to walk in the Word and with the Holy Spirit. A pilgrim had to travel to a far country, but he didn't know the way. But he had a map, and he also had a personal Guide to travel with. After a little while he said to himself, 'I am quite an intelligent fella graduated from university with good grades. I think I just need the map'. Then on looking round the Guide had disappeared. A few days later he found himself in the dead of night with it pouring down with rain and not able to see. He did not realise that he was heading for a precipice!

He did not know which direction to take. Suddenly he heard a still small voice (***Isaiah 30 vs 21***) which said '**Can I help you**?'. The Guide had returned! 'This is the way' he said, the pilgrim was so grateful.

After a while again he said to himself, 'you know I was silly worrying, I could have done it by myself'. Again, on looking round the Guide had left. A little while later the pilgrim found himself in a bog and was sinking with every step *(Proverbs 16 vs 18)* **Pride goes before a fall.** He then heard a still small voice again say **'Can I help you?'**. The Guide was back. The pilgrim said to the Guide would you like the map ... the Guide replied 'it was I that made it!'.

The map is the Bible and the Guide is the Holy Spirit, the Word and the Spirit always goes together.

Above – The team in Kitty

Page 48 & 49 - The work done on Amelia's compound in Kitty, Guyana

BEFORE

AFTER

DELIVERY TRUCK

THE NEW GATE

While I was in Guyana, I went into the interior to meet the Amerindians. It amazed me how hungry they were to hear the word of the Lord. They would travel in their canoes in the pitch darkness just to get to the meeting. A wonderful, hungry people for the gospel. I have already mentioned that I grew up with 'clean dirt' as my Mother used to say, I was never sick, just skinny as a boy which stood me in good stead when I visited them. It didn't come as a shock to sleep on the floor with creepy crawlies.

The Amerindians have a wonderful way of life! Just give them a chainsaw and they will build you a church in no time at all. As a white man I had to be careful not to frighten the children. At one village we went to I was mucking about shouting out 'Wahoo' and they started to scream! Were they screaming because I was so good looking? I don't think so, as they were terrified as I had screwed up my face! You need wisdom as they had never seen a white man before. *If any of you lacks wisdom, let him ask of God, who gives to all liberally and without reproach, and it will be given to him. (James 1vs 5 NKJV)*. In training for reigning, on the job training as you go*! I will instruct you and teach you in the way you should go; (Psalm 32:8 NIVUK).*

Top: Pastor Melvin & Shem the Guide in the Amerindians' Church

Bottom: Everday life in the jungle.

Top: Life in the Amerindian village
Bottom Left: Reg on his way to the village
Bottom Right: Shem the Guide

Do you believe in angels? I do. I believe that there are myriads and myriads of good angels who are given charge over God's people. The writer of Hebrews tells us that angels are ministering spirits sent to serve those who will inherit salvation. (Hebrews 1:14) I am glad to know that wherever I go there is an angel of God that encamps around me, ready to rescue me. On my return to Kitty, the town where I was staying next to Sophia, I was walking back to where I was staying and as I went down the alleyway, which was the entrance, I suddenly felt the Holy Spirit say 'Stop!' As I stopped and turned my head to the right, a big guy put a blade across my jugular and tried to steal my ring! Foolishly I had left it on! Guyana is the sort of place where you don't want to look very prosperous! I was so angry, I didn't have time to be frightened and I said, 'In the Name of Jesus you are not going to do this, I forbid it!' I used the sword of the spirit, which is the Word of God I took authority over the situation. The man started trembling in fear and ran away with me still shouting 'JESUS'.

Here I was feeling 'What a mighty man of God' all puffed up!! Until the Lord spoke to me clearly and said 'Reg it wasn't you! I give my angels charge over *you'* **(Psalm 91 vs 11 'He will give His angels charge over you').** I can't emphasise enough the power and authority that we have in Jesus when we put it on our tongue and speak it out! Then and only then will you see action. No Word no life! *In the beginning was the Word, and the Word was with God, and the Word was God' (John 1 vs 1).* Jesus is the Word; the Holy Spirit is the power. One without the other doesn't work. Only the Word and Spirit together. You can hear the Word all day long but if you don't put into action what you are hearing, faith without works is dead. *For as the body without the spirit is dead, so faith without works is dead also. (James 2:26).*

We also travelled to a town called Mahaicony to help Pastor Melvin build a church and purchase steel frames for the windows. I also had the privilege of baptising four people.

On the way to Mahaicony we had to pass through a place called Buxton. In Buxton the thieves had Kalashnikov rifles robbed people up on the main highway and then ran back into the jungle. I travelled through this area many times in a car which had no floor! You could actually see the road as you drove along. I had my feet on the chassis looking at the ground and hoped that my backside wouldn't touch the floor! I also had to hide as a white man so that the bandits wouldn't see me and attack us! Thank the Lord we arrived safely everytime.

Top: Baptism in Mahaicony
Bottom: Church under construction

Chapter 7

BREAD OF LIFE - CHURCH WITHOUT WALLS

On my return to London after my time in the Caribbean I found the River Church had closed the kitchen serving a hot breakfast for the poor and the homeless. I had run this with James, Thomas and Irene who were loyal, faithful servants who for many years had helped out in the background doing the cooking, washing up and preparation. We need to honour people like this for being the backbone to the ministry that people do not see.

I felt in my spirit to do the only thing I knew how; open a market stall underneath the flyover of the A13, serving tea, coffee, and sandwiches under the unction of the Holy Spirit. So, Bread of Life – Church without Walls was birthed. *Then Jesus declared, 'I am the bread of life. Whoever comes to me will never go hungry, and whoever believes in me will never be thirsty' (John 6:35 NIV). Taste and see that the Lord is good; (Psalm 34:8 NIV).* Our vision is to break down the partitions between denominations. We work on the premise of *Habbakuk*

2:2-3. I will leave you to look that one up. As always, a market trader for Jesus with my grandson called Thomas Miller, a good name for someone working for the Bread of Life church outreach.

Reg & daughter Deborah with the tea and sandwiches

Peter Churchill joined us from the Church without walls at Victoria, London as Pastor. A kind and generous man, very loving. A humble man who doesn't promote himself. If ever I have seen a pillar, a foundation stone for the church, it is Peter the rock. Reflecting the love of Jesus with his wife Wendy. The picture on page 59 is of me with Peter holding a tract we came across in the CLC Christian bookshop. We never ordered it we just found it on the shelf and felt it was confirmation from the Lord that He had put us together to outreach into the community on the streets. Peter is very easy to love, like Liz Stanley who has been with us from the start. Always available to reach out to those in need. (What a beautiful gift). As a nurse she works in a very practical way and uses her skills to show the love of Jesus. Alongside them there is Nigel Weekes who is the Youth Pastor of River Church who plays the bongos. It is no good just saying to a hungry man 'Jesus loves you' you need to feed him! If he is thirsty give him something to drink! *'In as much as you did it to one of the least of these, My brethren, you did it to Me.' (Matthew 25 :40 NKJV).* People don't care how much you know until they know how much you care.

Another long-time connection through Church without Walls is Kurt Erickson who has worked with the homeless for over 25 years in Victoria. He came to the UK from the USA in 1991 where he had been part of David Wilkerson's Time Square church in New York. He came with his wife Asha and together they founded Eleos Ministries in 1994 in Tower Hamlets. He has worked for over 20 years doing chaplaincy work in

Bethnal Green. He has two sons in the ministry, Adam who serves alongside him and Wesley who is at Bible College in America. Asha went home to be with the Lord about 10 years ago. He is a man after my own heart.

With Peter Churchill and the tract!

Chapter 8

MISSION TO AFRICA

The Bread of Life was invited to Ghana by Margaret Boateng, or Millie as we knew her, to see the work she was doing in Kintampo. Millie goes to the River Church in Canning Town. She had bought a large plantation which she had started from scratch. On it vegetables are grown and livestock kept. There are also brick buildings for storage and living quarters. The Lord had sent us to Kintampo as they needed a generator to pump water and to encourage Millie. At the same time the Lord had opened a door for us through her. We were there by divine appointment. Without Him we can do nothing *'I am the vine; you are the branches. If you remain in me and I in you, you will bear much fruit; apart from me you can do nothing.' (John 15:5 NIVUK).* When we travel abroad the 'seed', as in any money, that we carry is not spent on hotels or personal pleasure, it is given to help the brethren, the poor and those in need; The widow, orphans, prisoners and the sick. *'Truly I tell you, whatever you did for one of the least of these brothers and sisters of mine, you did for me.' (Matthew 25 vs 40 NIVUK)*. The Great Commission. ***In the same way, let your light shine before others, that they may see your good deeds and glorify your Father in heaven. (Matt 5 vs 16 NIVUK).*** In training for reigning!

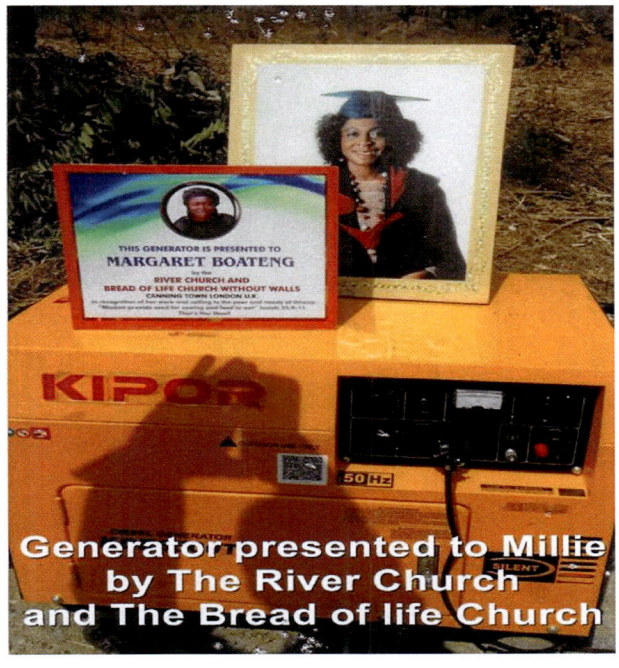

Millie returned to England, and I stayed behind in her family's compound. The Bible says that you are to look for a place and stay there ***'When you come to a town***

or village, go in and look for someone who is willing to welcome you, and stay with him until you leave that place.' (Matthew 10 vs 11 GNT). That has applied wherever I have been sent around the world. Again, I did not know anyone. I was waiting on instruction from the Lord. So, I went on walkabout like Crocodile Dundee in the wilderness. The Lord can direct you when you are moving by faith. Like a car when it is on the move it can be steered in the right direction. You need to take a step of faith and put your foot on the accelerator.

So here I was staying in a small town in the wilderness, very hot and dusty, quite sparse. I felt in my spirit to go into the local school where the children were sitting under a large shelter with no doors or windows and the walls were made from mud and breeze block. There were about 150 children grouped according to age, separated by mud block partitions most of them were in poor clothes and had worn out shoes, some had no shoes at all. Few had school uniforms. We decided to go to the local market and purchased over 30 pairs of second-hand shoes and we had the uniforms made locally. Praise the Lord!

I was greeted by the headmaster, who was also a pastor … he then introduced me to a visiting pastor's wife who in turn introduced me to Ebenezer, her husband. He had been sent from Accra to Kintampo after finishing Bible School. Our first calling as Bread of Life was to the children in need and the second was to help Pastor Ebenezer to build a church in the centre of the town.

To see the Lord at work was amazing. With just a patch of ground behind the shops on the main street we started to build. They told me that the Lord had told them that someone was on their way from England. I did not know where the money was coming from, but I knew that we were sent. I just kept using my 'flexible friend', my bank card, the money just kept coming out of my heavenly bank account. It was a situation reminiscent of the Prophet Elisha who helped the Widow woman in 2 Kings Chapter 4. As long as she kept pouring the oil into empty vessels the oil kept coming! This was strange for me as I still did not recognise at the time my apostolic anointing (a person sent). This word is taken from the Greek word 'Apostolos', which means 'messenger' or 'one sent with messages of hope'.

In Kintampo I met my spiritual son, his name was Ernest, I had to train him in the way of a market trader; how much one, how much two, how much three? Hoping to buy three for the price of two!! But I don't get offended if people say no! He used to drive me around as

FOUNTAIN GATE CHAPEL

FOUNTAIN GATE ACADEMY SCHOOL

Apostle Reggie assisted the below names of pupil in Fountain Gate Academy to acquire their basic needs and paid their school fees.

NAMES OF STUDENTS	SEX	AGE
1. Jessica Malmore	F	8
2. Wisdom Aba-am	M	16
3. Regina Akurugu	F	13
4. Zeku Prince	M	13
5. Pena Patricia	F	13
6. Alfred Brenya	M	8
7. Sulemana Latifa	F	11
8. Okrah Kinsford	M	7
9. Juliet Mbowila	F	3
10. Ishmael Donkor	M	8
11. Prince Dowana	M	8
12. Louisa Malmore	F	3
13. Fauzan Ansuma	M	3
14. Desmond Adoesom	M	8
15. Ofori Stephen	M	13

Thanks to the River Christian Centre and the Bread of Life church without walls .Canning Town London England E16 ILZ.
02074761171
APOSTLE RAGGIE.
reggie@riverchurch.org.uk

Pastor James Akanwi Akansi
Pastor, FGC
0243614467 / 0508270124
akansiakanwi@yahoo.com
Fountain Gate chapel
P.O BOX 144 Kintampo .Ghana

Lady Pastor Patience Tapena
Pastor, CEM
0207609914

Tweneboah Mensah
Headmaster
0500097108

Our Sincere gratitude to Apostle Reggie for the assistance

OUR VISION: To raise lively and purposeful churches of Jesus Christ, where 'people is our focus' and to demonstrate to the world the all sufficient God who makes rivers in the desert.

"Behold, I will do a new thing; now it shall spring forth; shall ye not know it? I will even make a way in the wilderness, and rivers in the desert" - Isaiah 43:19

W: fountaingatechapel.org

my taxi driver. When I met first met him, he was renting the car from someone else giving them the rent money with very little left for himself. I used to sit in the front, so that others could get in the back. That is how it works in Africa you try to pick up as many people as possible, as you pay so little for each trip, a mere 20p. On one particular day, a young man was helping a sick old man to get into the car. As the car stopped the power of God, the Holy Spirit fell, and I found myself getting out of the car with an anger against this Spirit of Infirmity I prayed for the man and he was then able to walk by himself! On enquiring who the man was I was told it was the local Muslim Imam. Later in the week we went to see him and prayed in the name of Jesus. Actions speak louder than words because the Lord watches over His Word to perform it. *(Jeremiah 1:12)*.

Ernest came to me one day after he had been driving me around and said 'Da' (because that is what he called me), 'My uncle wants to sell some land in the village'. I knew it was the Lord's hand. But we did not have all the money, so I told him to hold what we had in his hand and let his uncle see it and tell him 'This is all I have but you are welcome to it as I don't have any more to give you'. (In training for reigning one in the hand is worth two in the bush). The uncle took the money, the 'all that we had', and with the agreement of the elders in the village we purchased the land. On the land we have cashew trees growing freely, pigs that we purchased later, vegetables, things that meet the needs of the poor. Ernest today has his own taxi, and he can take the products to market as well as pick up people. God's work, done God's way, gets God's supply. When you honour the Lord, the Lord honours you.

The Lord also gave me a spiritual daughter called Georgina, who we met in the local restaurant. She worked cleaning pots and pans but was treated very badly. They worked staff as hard as they could, then got rid of them and got fresh labour in every month. She had a baby on her back, and I felt the Lord wanted me to give her a little something with a message that the Lord saw her plight. Next time we went, she wasn't there, and I asked my spiritual son if he knew where she was, and he took me to her. 'Georgina' I said, 'Do you have a table?' Being a market trader, I wanted to set up a market stall for her as we had done already for others in Accra on the side of the road two or three years earlier. Here we were now in Kintampo, twelve hours from Accra the capital of Ghana. She said no Daddy (they all called me Daddy!) but then I felt the Lord speak to me; 'ask her to take you to the place where she is living'. Right in the centre of her village outside her front door was a very large clay oven, as big as a room and probably older than me! I was 60 then. I told her 'You are going to make bread; do you know anyone that knows how?' She said, 'yes, the lady

that I am living with'. I am sure that is why we are called the Bread of Life today **Oh, taste and see that the Lord is good; (Psalm 34:8).** We had to buy the grain and take it to the mill to get it ground with all the other ingredients. We were now making bread for the poor, with land to grow food and livestock! That is the God we serve; the best is yet to come. Amen!

This happened at the same time as we were trying to build a church. I am not surprised that I was actually out there for a few months. Our gifts in the natural we sometimes don't realise have been given by the Lord, so He uses that gift for His Glory. When I returned to England my bank account was still in credit. That is the Lord we serve! There is a song which always comes to mind **'Jesus makes a way where there seems to be no way'. (Don Moen ©1991 Reg's version).**

As Bread of Life, we don't sow seed into barren ground only in fertile soil. The Bread of Life needs wisdom as we don't give handouts, we give hands up. As the Lord gives people dignity. We always look for those that are trying to make a living to help themselves in some way for example collecting plastic bottles, 'Give them a fish and they will eat the fish, give them a fishing rod and let them fish for themselves.' You need a lot of wisdom as a sent one. **'The harvest is plentiful, but the workers are few. Ask the Lord of the harvest, therefore, to send out workers into his harvest field. (Luke 10 vs 2 NIVUK).**

While in Ghana we were able to bless another Pastor, who was trying to build a church. This story illustrates how we need wisdom when we do the Lord's work. We gave him the money in sterling but instead of going to the Bank he went to the money launderers on the street because we would get more money in exchange. We had contaminated the 'seed' because the money that goes through the money exchangers hands is used for prostitution, drug dealing and theft.

Because of this the church was never completed. The Lord could not honour that, and we needed to repent!

Georgina the Baker with Ernest the Farmer, and the bread oven!

Chapter 9

MISSION TO ISRAEL

The next mission was to Israel. As I didn't know anyone, I made enquiries of a few people but to no avail. I found out why later: I had to take that step of faith. I knew in Israel that Derek Prince had spent his last days at Christ Church in Jerusalem just behind the Jaffa Gate opposite King David's Museum. So, I went there first. I met Chas and Dave from America in the Christian bookshop next door, not the Chas and Dave of cockney East End music fame. Chas introduced me to the Messianic Believers on the Jaffa Rd where I was able to do some street evangelism in Tel Aviv. We got chased out by the orthodox Jews into the red light district. It was even better witnessing there alongside Elieser a Messianic Jew from South America who had made Aliyah. (Aliyah is when a Jew moves to Israel and becomes an Israeli citizen). An amazing opportunity for us to witness to the prostitutes standing outside their little rooms or dropping tracts through the doors if they weren't there.

On my return to Jerusalem, I stayed in the International Hotel opposite King David's gate. I still hadn't met or made any connections with the Palestinian believers in Jesus, so I decided to go on walkabout again like Crocodile Dundee. I found a cathedral within a short distance of the hotel. That is where I decided to go for the Sunday service. Sunday came round and I left the hotel but must have turned left instead of right and found myself lost. I stood in the road and said to the Lord, 'I am lost'. A man walked across the road, I said to him 'Can you tell me where I can find the Cathedral? He said, 'I don't know where the cathedral is but if you go through that gap behind you and up the stairs through the door you will find a service'. Then the man just disappeared! I followed his directions. As I entered and sat at the back the words on the screen said, 'Bread of Life'. I knew that I was in the right place which made me smile. Could the man who had appeared and disappeared have been an angel? **'The steps of a good man are ordered by the Lord' (Psalm 37 vs 23 NIVUK).** Just how did I know that it was an angel? If there was a cathedral in Canning Town everyone would know where it was as it is a big building and not a church hall. He had said to me 'I don't know of any cathedral' because he was sent to direct me! I wasn't lost I just thought I was! At the meeting they started to sing 'What a friend we have in Jesus' which is one of the two songs we always sing at the Bread of Life - Church without Walls on the street to the homeless, the needy and the lost at the Canning Town outreach on a Sunday morning. Here in Jerusalem this was a Baptist church that the Lord had led me to. I was able to share my vision with them of reaching the lost at any cost, they invited me to Bethlehem, but I didn't know how to get there.

The next day they sent a taxi for me, and it took about 30 – 40 minutes to get to Bethlehem from Jerusalem. You had to show your passports on the way because you were going into the Palestinian Territories. Two men met me as we arrived in Bethlehem. The director Bishara who founded the Bible School and Sari the director of The Shepherd Society. This was the beginning of the outreach to the Palestinian believers in Jesus. The Lord gave me another spiritual son, Issa, who had fled the West Bank for Bethlehem to try and make a new life for himself. His family had been silver smiths going back many generations. This was another situation where I was able to fulfil the scripture again *'In as much as you did it to one of the least of these, My brethren, you did it to Me.' (Matthew 25 :40)* because he was a Palestinian believer in Jesus.

Just before I had left for Israel the Lord had told me to take off my Messianic rings which have a Star of David with a Cross on top as I was travelling into the

Top left: Eliesar and his wife   Top right: with Chas & Dave

Bottom: with Israeli soldiers, the Lord does indeed encamp His angels around us!

Palestinian district where there were lots of anti-Jewish posters. This reminds me of a time when I got arrested on the Temple Mount in Jerusalem because they thought that I was Jewish. It is wise to listen to the Lord even if you don't know or understand why at the time. Only Muslims are allowed to visit the mosque on a Friday and Saturday, I had just followed the crowds through the old city of Jerusalem not realising they were all Muslims that were going to the Temple Mount!

The Bread of Life was called to Israel to be the cement between the Palestinian believers in Jesus and the Jewish believers in Yeshua. The key is found in Ezekiel 47: 22-23 *'You are to allot it as an inheritance for yourselves and for the foreigners residing among you and who have children. You are to consider them as native-born Israelites; along with you they are to be allotted an inheritance among the tribes of Israel. In whatever tribe a foreigner resides, there you are to give them their inheritance,' declares the Sovereign Lord. (NIVUK)* As Christian believers from outside Israel we are called to be the cement with the gift of reconciliation (the sent ones). Bread of Life Church Without Walls, pulling down partitions between the denominations. Any friend of Jesus is a friend of mine. The Lord gave me a picture of a butterfly. Apparently, they mean peace. Jesus said, *'Blessed are the peacemakers, for they shall be called sons of God' (Matthew 5:9).* My spiritual son, Issa, made us some beautiful silver badges with the Bread of Life Church without Walls logo that we can wear as a thank you. We were also able to make a badge for Jonathan Croft on his visit to Israel from Kingdom Faith London, one of Colin Urquhart's satellite churches, as a thank you for visiting the House of Hope for children with learning difficulties run by my friend Salim, who is the director. They also have a manufacturing factory on the ground floor making brushes to help finance the children at the House of Hope, in Bethlehem.

One of the workers who makes brushes is blind. He works in the workshop beneath the school. Volunteers are always welcome to help in a practical way to help look after the children with Down's Syndrome. We are always looking for younger missionaries supported by their local church who are in training for reigning for missions.

On one of my return trips to Israel, still trying to work things out for myself, I was worried I would not make it into the Palestinian territories as everything stops as soon as it gets dark, and I thought I would get stuck in Jerusalem which is expensive. As a missionary I don't like to waste the Lord's money on hotels if I can help it.

Arriving by tube at Baker Street Station, in London, to catch the coach to Luton Airport I met a man who said he lived in Jerusalem and was on the same flight. He said that he could help me. On arrival at Ben Gurion Airport, Tel Aviv he told me to wait as he was going to give me a lift. I thought the lift was to just be to Jerusalem and he had somewhere for me to stay (Reggie working things out). As I stood there waiting, around the corner came a car with the emblem of the United Nations on it. 'Jump in', he said, 'I am taking you straight through to the Palestinian Territories'. Wow! As Chuck Missler, one of the best Bible teachers who has now gone home to the Lord, always said 'Wow' 'I said 'Wow, the Lord had done it again!' On our journey I asked him if he was married and had a family. 'No' He said, 'I am gay', that may worry some people but not me as I have never met anyone by accident. He said 'I am looking for a man' that opened a door for me to share the good news! And I had to tell him that I knew a Man who would never let him down, who was very faithful, and his name was Jesus. Now I had his attention, I gave him the gospel all the way on the journey to where I was staying in Bethlehem. Bashaa and Sari, the directors of the Bible School and Shepherd's Society, were there to greet us on our arrival. The gay man, who will remain nameless, promised to return and he did.

Once before I had a divine appointment with a homosexual on an Easyjet flight to Northern Ireland when I was on my way to visit Maghaberry prison. When you are witnessing to homosexuals, they like to think they are different. But when you explain to them that as far as the Lord is concerned, sexual sin is sexual sin whether you are gay or straight and all is forgivable. ***If we confess our sins, he is faithful and just and will forgive us our sins and cleanse us from all unrighteousness. (1 John 1 vs 9 NIVUK)***

If you go to Israel, you can see thousands of sheep and hundreds of shepherds at the water hole. When the shepherd leaves the water hole only his sheep follow him. An amazing thing to see. There are good shepherds and there are bad shepherds how can you know the difference? Here is another modern-day parable. In England and around the globe they use collie dogs to drive the sheep and they snap at the sheep's heels. The sheep are driven by fear. The good shepherd uses the slingshot as he leads his sheep, he doesn't drive them. He has a crooked staff in his hand, it is a long and sturdy stick with a hook at one end, often with the point flared outwards, to catch his sheep and stop them from getting into trouble. In addition, the crook may help to defend against attack by predators. The crook is also an aid to help balance the shepherd as he walks over rough terrain. ***Even though I walk through the darkest valley, I will fear no evil for you are with me; your rod and your staff, they comfort me. (Psalm 23:4 NIVUK)***

Have you ever seen a picture of Jesus carrying a lamb around his neck? I have often used this modern-day parable when talking to people who are hurting. The shepherd if he sees one of his sheep go astray will put a small stone in his sling or catapult and hit the ground in front of the sheep so that it won't go any further. Then if the sheep still doesn't stop, he hits the sheep on the nose with the second stone and that is painful! If then the sheep doesn't stop, and this sounds very cruel, he goes over to the sheep and breaks one of its hind legs. He will then pick that sheep up and carry that sheep until it has completely healed. When he puts that sheep down that sheep will never go far from the shepherd! ***My sheep know my voice (John 10 vs 4)***

The Good Shepherd – Nathan Greene
www.nathangreene.com

Sometimes the Lord has to do the same with us. He is not out to spoil our fun, but he knows the pain that we are letting ourselves in for.

Deliverance and healing are the children's bread, and working with gypsy Johnnie Barr, who could move immediately from the flesh to the spirit, from the natural to the supernatural as he knew his authority in Jesus and authority is greater than power. I repeat this; a 5ft 7 policeman, a 20 ton truck coming down the road it could flatten him. But he has the authority of the Queen of England, when he steps out into the road, he knows that that lorry must stop! How much more when we say stop! We have the authority of the Lord of Lords and the King of Kings and all the Heavenly hosts.

It is not 'I' that lives but Christ that lives in me, the hope of glory! I love to go into old Jerusalem and see the history, 'His story,' as many of us can testify as we walk through the Bible on our highway of holiness. The latest news from Bethlehem is that we have also been able to establish a carpenter's shop, as Jesus was a carpenter, and He is looking for joiners! (Get it?) The carpenter we met in Bethlehem was struggling but he made beautiful souvenirs from wood, he just needed a hand up. This is what the Bread of Life is called to do, to look after fellow believers. Especially in the Palestinian Territory of

Bethlehem which used to be 40% Christian but now there are only about 10% even though they have a refugee camp that the Shepherd society supports showing them the love of Jesus. On my return to the UK, I received information of a Muslim family of five fleeing the West Bank after becoming Christians. They were fleeing for their lives and are now in Bethlehem. They had to leave everything behind, their home and everything in it. Bread of Life Church without walls together with a member of the River church (who by the way has a Muslim husband), gave £500 - that is a witness to the Muslims showing them the love of Jesus. People don't care how much you know until they know how much you care. ***Then the King will say to those on His right hand, 'Come, you blessed of My Father, inherit the kingdom prepared for you from the foundation of the world: for I was hungry and you gave Me food; I was thirsty and you gave Me drink; I was a stranger and you took Me in; I was naked and you clothed Me; I was sick and you visited Me; I was in prison and you came to Me.'***

"Then the righteous will answer Him, saying, 'Lord, when did we see You hungry and feed You, or thirsty and give You drink? When did we see You a stranger and take You in, or naked and clothe You? Or

when did we see You sick, or in prison, and come to You?' And the King will answer and say to them, 'Assuredly, I say to you, in as much as you did it to one of the least of these My brethren, you did it to Me.' (Matthew 25 vs 34 -40 NKJV).*

We were able to buy 5 mattresses after finding them shelter. If we think about Christianity and Islam and the roots of both faiths, we can go back to the Scriptures and the book of Genesis. Isaac and Ishmael, the Lord loved both; one was the son of the promise and one of the flesh. **'And as for Ishmael, I have heard you. Behold, I have blessed him, and will make him fruitful (Genesis 19:20)** Once a person has received the life of Christ. Jesus tries to get us to see that it is not the first birth that counts but the second. He does not accept our first birth in Adam He accepts our second birth in Christ. (John 3 vs 3-5). We must be born again. Flesh gives birth to flesh and the spirit gives birth the spirit. What happens in the natural is closely connected to the spiritual. This has always from the beginning been a struggle. Cain and Able, Isaac and Ishmael, Jacob and Esau, Jesus and Adam. When heaven hits earth miracles happen. This is what happened to this Muslim family.

I had returned to England with no money. I still had to learn to try not to work things out for myself. I needed to learn to be like Pastor Thomas Watt of Prison Fellowship International in Barbados who just chuckled. We had no regular givers, and we still don't to this day. We totally rely on the Lord to supply all our needs according to His riches in glory. *(Philippians 4 vs 19).* I received a letter from Aviva the Insurance company to say they were looking for me and was I Reginald Gardner. I found out they had £20,000 for me. Even to this day I don't know where it came from, but I know a Man that does! Hallelujah!

Palestinian Outreach

Top left – Bismara, Director of the Bible School

Bottom – Sari, Director of the Shepherd Society

They both invited me to Bethlehem.

Our carpenter in Bethlehem attached to the Bread of Life Church without Walls.

Chapter 10

MISSION TO NORTHERN IRELAND

Because of my connection with Prison Fellowship International it opened the doors for me to go to Northern Ireland and visit Maghaberry High Security prison. One of the members of Prison Fellowship International in Northern Ireland was a chap called Ray McGibbon and he was training to be a priest. He took me to Maghaberry, and the amazing thing was that they gave me an electric key which opened ALL the prison doors. I was able to walk around freely and minister to those that had been sentenced to life imprisonment. I was called to speak to long term prisoners who were inside for murder, shooting and other violent crimes such as bombings. The prisoners were IRA and UDF terrorists. This was the time of the so called 'Troubles'.

It is amazing how God works. On my way out I went to hand in the electric key at the guard room and they wanted to know 'How did you get this? You are supposed to have high security clearance', which I didn't have, with references! all I had said was that I had come to visit. The following story from the book of Acts in the New Testament comes to mind. The church at the time were praying fervently for Peter who was in prison and an angel walked in and tapped him on the side and said, 'Get up' Peter did not know if he was dreaming but his chains fell off. The angel walked Peter out of the prison, and he suddenly found himself outside. When he knocked on the door of the church that was praying fervently for him to be set free, the girl who opened the door could not believe her eyes. She closed the door and went to tell the saints praying that Peter was outside, but they said she must have seen a ghost. These were the people that had been fervently praying! Sometimes I wonder if they had been praying more in 'hope' than 'faith'. ***'To have faith is to be sure of the things we hope for, to be certain of the things we cannot see.' (Hebrews 11 vs 1).*** I thought to myself if God can get Peter out of prison, then I am not surprised that he had got me in! As a 'sent one' the Lord will open the doors for you. Apostle is not a title it is a calling and there is the miracle, the fact that I was there!

Like Paul I have learned to be all things to all men. ***'To the weak I became weak, to win the weak. I have become all things to all people so that by all possible*** *means I might save some.' (1 Corinthians 9:22 NIVUK)*. It is not a big deal but there is the miracle! The ordinary becomes the extraordinary, the Lord is so supernaturally natural! He will use you at different times in all the gifts, it doesn't mean I am a healer or an apostle or a pastor in the true sense of the word, but I am an Ambassador for Christ with the evangelistic gift of the street pastor that moves in the apostolic, in other words I am a child of God. Amen! It is not a question of capability but availability.

Chapter 11

MISSION TO LITHUANIA

David Gill had invited me to go with him on a trip to Lithuania. I asked the Lord what His purpose was for me to go out there. Two ladies had already set up an outreach to the poor and homeless. Their ministry was well established, and it had been going for many years. They had established a good supply of food. The only need that they had was that they needed money to pay their staff. But I just felt in my spirit that was not the calling for the Bread of Life Church without Walls.

On this occasion I felt that the Lord had plans for us to support the local drug rehabilitation centre there. It was run on the same lines as Teen Challenge. This is a ministry birthed by David Wilkerson in New York. The story can be found in the book 'The Cross and the Switchblade'. Back in London I had been involved with Teen Challenge. Teen Challenge helps men and women dependent on drugs quit for God. They first came to my attention through Harry Baldwin, who I had worked with alongside Johnny Barr in Canning Town. We had both joined his church about the same time in the early 1990's. Harry had met a brother working as a manager in a shoe shop by the name of Javier, who the Lord had called to start a Teen Challenge Rehab Centre in Ilford. The place they had planned to use was in a terrible condition when they first saw it but would be large enough to accommodate 18 men when restored. Another one of God's miracles as they were able to purchase the building for £1. Harry Baldwin did all the plastering. He was a master craftsman, one of the best in London, out of Bethnal Green.

Teen Challenge in the UK drive buses to various places to find people that want to join their Drug Rehab programme so they can be set free from addiction. The Lord was doing the same thing in Lithuania as they had a rehab house for forty men. They asked me to share a Word which they videoed and streamed on their TV channel. I spoke on, 'Hurt people hurt people' and forgiveness. To illustrate I told the story of the naughty monkey (told previously in this book) about letting go and forgiveness.

They had a bus, but it was an absolute rust bucket! It needed new tyres, new everything! The Lord had given me a vision to sow a seed for them to establish a fundraising fund for them to raise the money to buy a new bus. *Now he who supplies seed to the sower and bread for food will also supply and increase your store of seed and will enlarge the harvest of your righteousness. (2 Corinthians 9:10 NIVUK) Jesus said "Which of you, if your son asks for bread, will give him a stone? (Matthew 7:9 NIVUK).*

Chapter 12

RECENT ADVENTURES

While working on this book I was rushed into hospital. I spent four days hooked up to this heart machine with wires attached to my chest. It is amazing how the Lord uses situations for His purposes. As here was I attached to a heart monitor while all around me was chaos. There were only four beds in the ward and opposite was a poor man saying 'No, No!' tormented in his sleep. Another patient who would not stay in bed, he kept trying to leave and struggling with the nurses. One night it was particularly horrendous as the day staff had given him a 'Micky Finn' (injection). That knocked him out for the day, but the trouble was when the night staff came on duty, he was wide awake! I was supposed to be resting!

Because of the excitement my heart machine was going through the roof! The nurse was telling me to relax, the man opposite was shouting 'No, No, No!' and I wanted to disconnect the heart machine and the wires and lay my hands on the patients. As I prayed I felt in my spirit the Lord say 'No as you would make things worse'. **1 Timothy 5 vs 22 'Do not lay hands on anyone hastily'.**

After being in the deliverance ministry for a number of years I was used to people coming for help. The staff in the hospital knew that I was born again, and I was feeling very disappointed as faith without works is dead. ***James 2 vs 14-20***. But I had to remember that I was not on the street or at a deliverance meeting I was in hospital! The Lord is so gracious as that evening I felt in my spirit just to reach out with my arms extended as the chap who was trying to escape passed by with all the staff chasing him. He stopped at the bottom of my bed. With my hands outstretched he grasped both of them, so I drew him to me. Remember I am still laying there with the wires attached and now I had his head on my chest. Then I was able to just put my hands on his head and pray the love of Jesus into him. He just went quiet. It is not always demonic influences that we have to pray against sometimes they just need the love of Jesus. After 30 years I had learned something that I will never forget! Amen!

In training for reigning means loving the person but hating the sin ***1 Peter 4 vs 8***. This was a tremendous witness to the Muslim staff demonstrating the power of the Holy Spirit and the love of Jesus.

As well as ministering to the patients I was also able to encourage the nurses and sisters who were born again believers. As Christians it is difficult to administer God's grace when you are a member of staff. I think they call it political correctness. One of the sisters was very concerned that she was not able to get to church. I had to explain to her, 'you are the church, it is not about the building it is about the body of Christ! They weren't there by accident that is where the Lord has put them to administer His grace as their very presence makes a difference.

Chapter 13

REFLECTIONS ON 30 YEARS OF SERVICE

Looking back over 30 years and now understanding that our steps are ordered of the Lord. Alone but never lonely. Sharing God's faithfulness to encourage those who feel that they are called to reach out. It has to start where you are. For me that was Canning Town, London, my Jerusalem with five years on the streets. Giving out tracts, engaging with the homeless on a one to one basis. Then Africa with Patience in Accra, setting her up with a stall on the road. Georgina in Kintampo with her clay oven. Ernest, the Lord bought the land with cashew trees. ***The Lord is my shepherd, I lack nothing (Psalm 23 vs 1 NIV).*** Bread of Life Church without walls pulling down the partitions between the denominations. ***Which of you, if your son asks for bread, will give him a stone? (Matthew 7:9) Oh, taste and see that the Lord is good (Psalm 34:8)*** This book is testimony to that goodness.

How odd of God to choose the Jews! But not so 'odd' as those who choose a Jewish God. Jesus was a carpenter and is looking for joiners, no electric tools in those days, just big muscles! In my youth I loved the stories of Jesus healing the sick. Later as a Christian I was drawn to the synagogue in Westcliff, Essex wishing to be a part of the Jewish fraternity. A few years later I had an opportunity to go inside when one of my very good friends died. Going back now I remember, at the age of 15, I got the opportunity to work in a menswear outfitter. Years later, a Jewish man, who was a highly successful supplier of famous brands such as Jacques Vert to large department stores, came to me and said why didn't I run my own business. At that stage I was the manager of one of Harry Fenton's Menswear shops. He said to me 'if you come to me, I will let you have all the returns that are sent back from the shop for £1 a garment'. That was the beginning of my market days which allowed me to buy Captain Bligh's house in Swanley village and my first Rolls Royce. So, in a way I grew up with the Jewish fraternity.

I like Rock and Roll, as long as I am standing on the Rock (Jesus) and my Name is on the Roll (Salvation). At the age of 51 to find that wealth doesn't bring you happiness, missing out on my children growing up. Today smiling as my daughter Deborah and I are often asked if we are Jewish by other Jews. We always reply, 'only by circumcision of the heart'.

Reg with his daughter Deborah

We must be careful that we do not get into idolatry. We are called to make them jealous of their Messiah. At the age of 82 in a few months I can honestly say it has been a wonderful journey from a street kid to a street pastor into the apostolic ministry travelling halfway around the world over these last 30 years. The Bread of

Life Church without Walls is still reaching out being the cement as Christians between the Jewish Messianic Believers in Yeshua and the Palestinian believers in Jesus. *"Thus, you shall divide this land among yourselves according to the tribes of Israel. It shall be that you will divide it by lot as an inheritance for yourselves, and for the strangers who dwell among you and who bear children among you. They shall be to you as native-born among the children of Israel; they shall have an inheritance with you among the tribes of Israel. And it shall be that in whatever tribe the stranger dwells, there you shall give him his inheritance," says the Lord God. (Ezekiel 47:21-23).*

'And if a stranger dwell with you in your land, you shall not mistreat him. The stranger who dwells among you shall be to you as one born among you, and you shall love him as you were strangers in the land of Egypt: I am the Lord your God.

'You shall do no injustice in judgment, in measurement of length, weight, or volume. (Leviticus 19:33-35)

These messages from the scripture are what we bring to pull down the partitions between them as the Bread of Life Church without Walls.

It is now 30 years since my trip down to Snodland in Kent. Here I am in Canning Town with a church whose roots go back 125 years. 125 years of outreach to the poor. First as the Docklands Settlement Board, then the Mayflower Centre under Alan Craig, now the River Church Mission Centre under the Rev. David Gill. David who laid down his ministry as Senior Pastor to allow a brother from Johnny Barr's church, (after Johnny had gone home to be with the Lord), to come over on the Macedonian Call with administration skills to negotiate with Newham Council on the development of the site for the future. The Lord restored Rev David Gill's ministry as Senior Pastor, with Melanie his wife opening a large nursery on site. Reaching out into the community showing the love of Jesus, with the Bread of Life church without walls, having a hot food bank for the children in need in Guyana run by her mother Amelia.

Be encouraged, as this book is for you and a testimony to God's faithfulness! '

Then the Lord replied:

***"Write down the revelation
and make it plain on tablets
so that a herald may run with it.***

> *For the revelation awaits an appointed time;*
> > *it speaks of the end*
> > *and will not prove false.*
> *Though it linger, wait for it;*
> > *it will certainly come*
> > *and will not delay.*
>
> *Habbakuk 2:2-3 .*

We now minister where others have gone before. As the Body of Christ in Canning Town, London the Lord makes a way for our gifts and has given us the ministry of reconciliation. *'For I know the plans I have for you,' declares the Lord, 'plans to prosper you and not to harm you, plans to give you hope and a future. Then you will call on me and come and pray to me, and I will listen to you. You will seek me and find me when you seek me with all your heart.' (Jeremiah 29 vs 11 – 13 NIV),* but we still have to choose. Katherine Kulman received her healing ministry after two men turned it down. Like Deborah in the Bible said to the men *'if I go, you will not get the glory' (Judges 4:9)* It is a tragedy today that men don't want to take their rightful place. Right from the very beginning in Genesis 1 vs 28, Adam just stood there beside Eve, when he could have said "no", what did the devil take from Adam and Eve! Jesus in the wilderness, "if you will bow down and worship me, I will give you all the kingdoms of the World" Where did Satan get the Kingdoms from? Jesus went to the Cross and said, "It is finished". Question "What did he take back?" Then what did Jesus give back to His church? **The authority**. "Did God really say?" Satan is still trying to plant doubt today. It is important to know the Word. Jesus said "It is written". Gladys Aylward left for China from the London City Mission in the East End of London even though they told her she wasn't suitable! Her story was told in the film "The Inn of the Sixth Happiness". A powerful testimony. ***"For many are called, but few are chosen."*** Matthew 22:14 (NKJV) As you have to be determined "Remember that I have commanded you to be determined and confident! Do not be afraid or discouraged, for I, the Lord your God, am with you wherever you go." (Josh 1:5 GNT). If the Lord has given you a vision, stick to it.

I would like to expand on the remarks about the Word and the Spirit as one is never without the other. In Genesis 1 vs 2 -3 it says that the Spirit hovers over the waters. The Lord said let there be light and there was light. Evangelists are called to demonstrate signs and wonders to an unbelieving world. The Holy Spirit hovers over the world and waits to confirm His Word with signs and wonders following the Word. Evangelists are the only ones who are called to an unbelieving world to move in this ministry of His demonstration and power. Jesus was both. That does not mean that we are NOT called to move at times in the five-fold ministry: Apostles, prophets, evangelists, teachers and pastors.

I am a street pastor to the unbelieving world, and I have learned to stay within my calling. As street pastors we are really evangelists that can move in the gift of the pastoral ministry when necessary. The point I am trying to make is that signs and wonders are for unbelievers as they can see and experience the power of God. Especially in the area of healing. Now for the church, on the other hand, signs and wonders always follow the Word. This is a safeguard against false signs and wonders as the enemy comes as an angel of light with the counterfeit and people start looking for the miracles, signs and wonders before waiting for the Word. They end up following man instead of Jesus and the Holy Spirit. The devil doesn't counterfeit 10 bob notes anymore because they are not in circulation, but when the real thing is about counterfeit is about and we need to realise that not all signs and wonders are from the Lord as the devil comes as an angel of light.

The Lord will take you on a journey at times not knowing where you are going. ***If any of you lacks wisdom, you should ask God, who gives generously to all without finding fault, and it will be given to you. (James 1:5)*** Others will reap what you have sown. I like to say that may be one day I'll meet the person who brought Billy Graham to the Lord, one of the best evangelists of the 20th century. ***For the saying is true, 'Someone plants, someone else reaps.' I have sent you to reap a harvest in a field where you did not work; others worked there, and you profit from their work." (John 4 vs 37/38 GNT).*** Sowing and reaping history is 'his story' of God's faithfulness and there have been lots of testimonies of God's faithfulness in this book. Also it is testimony to His grace. G.R.A.C.E. God's Riches At Christ's Expense. Please forgive me for indulgence as I look back over the years. Growing up like the Artful Dodger in Oliver Twist. Always knowing the presence of the Lord even as a small boy. The closeness of Jesus and loving the stories of His life here on Earth. Running to Him when I was in trouble. Everything seems to have a connection. Captain Bligh's house, the story of Mr Christian on the Mutiny on the Bounty. Using the cellars in the house to hold stocks of clothes instead of barrels of wine. The replica slave ship from the film that was docked at Tower Bridge, in London where I had the pleasure of sharing the good news with the visitors. Celebrating 200 years of the emancipation of the slave trade. William Wilberforce who fought as a young man to stop slavery as a member of parliament. Coming back from the West Indies and Guyana, South America after asking them to forgive us as a nation. Able to share on their national TV. Their heroes, Cuffy with his statue in Kitty, Guyana. Bussa in Bridgetown, Barbados. The leaders of the uprising. Because slave blood was spilled the Lord gave them the whole of the Caribbean to for rule for themselves. The Lord called me to the Docklands settlement in the East End of London in 1994. Now celebrating 125 years of reaching out to the local area over the years. These are our roots and now it is one of the most expensive areas in London to live. The vision is to go into all the world! The Lord has given this vision to the Rev David Gill, a humble man, walking in his father, Pastor Russ's footsteps. Pastor Russ has retired now and like me we are praying for younger missionaries.

This is history (which is His-story) of how He cares for the less fortunate through His church, His 'sent ones' the Body of Christ. *(Jeremiah 29 vs 11-13). For I know the plans I have for you,' declares the Lord, 'plans to prosper you and not to harm you, plans to give you hope and a future. Then you will call on me and come and pray to me, and I will listen to you. You will seek me and find me when you seek me with all your heart.* Going on to fulfil the Great Commission. Chuck Colson, President Nixon's Aide, on coming out of prison started Angel Tree for Christmas where people donate gifts for the children of prisoners. It is now known as Prison Fellowship International. Working with Thomas Watts, the director of Prison Fellowship International in Barbados and around the Caribbean. Visiting prisoners and seeing many come to Christ. The miracle of being able to take pictures in the prison as a testimony to God's greatness and goodness. Jesus makes a way where there seems to be no way. He works in ways we cannot see; He will make a way for me and for you!

Working with Owen Williams of the Bible Society and at one time witnessing to and seeing 66 prisoners coming to Christ over two visits to a prison in St Vincent. One for each book of the Bible. Wonderful to again be able to take pictures of the inmates. Living testimony to how the Lord opens doors, as in Northern Ireland with an electronic key card, we were able to open every door in Maghaberry prison high security prison to share the gospel with bombers and murderers serving life sentences for their crimes. The Lord got Peter in the Bible out of prison, so he got the Bread of Life into the prison (Acts

12). Is anything too difficult for the Lord? *I am the Lord, the God of all mankind. Is anything too hard for me? (Jeremiah 32 vs 27 NIVUK).* Security wanted to know who let us in without getting clearance and who gave me the plastic electronic key? Could it have been an angel? Maybe one day I will find out!